Barbra Streisand Christmas Memories

Piano/vocal arrangements by John Nicholas, Justin Pyne, and Peggy White.

Photography (Ms. Streisand): Firooz Zahedi
Photography (Still Life): Ian Logan

ISBN 1-57560-572-4

Visit our website at www.cherrylane.com

I had finished recording all of the songs for this album when September 11th, 2001, happened. The United States…indeed, our world…would never be the same. Thousands of lives were lost…and millions of lives were changed on that tragic morning.

In the days after, we witnessed many acts of heroism—men and women risking their lives to come to the aid of others. We saw their faces on television…people of all colors…all faiths…all the nationalities that make up America. We listened to their voices…resilient and proud. (Those New York accents never sounded so beautiful!)

To all who grieve for those who have perished…may you celebrate their precious lives with gratitude for the time you had together…knowing they will live in your memory forever.

With hope and love,

Barbra

'Tis the season...

The late afternoon sun casts a filigree of shimmering diamonds across the cobalt ocean. Below the rocky cliffs, foamy waters break gently upon the footprint-soft sand. In the distance, kids on surfboards wait patiently for the ultimate ride back to shore. Fishing boats bob to and fro in the Pacific breeze. At the edge of the horizon, twenty-six miles away, the hills of Catalina Island appear like a hazy mirage. Above the bluff sits a magical rose garden...fragrant perfume fills the air. In this idyllic-summer postcard setting, Barbra Streisand is putting together her first collection of Christmas songs in 3½ decades. Her delightful guest cottage by the sea has temporarily been transformed into an enchanting recording studio.

It's somewhat ironic that our most beloved Christmas songs have usually been written and recorded in temperatures well above those found in Santa's arctic village. The reason, of course, is simple. The rules of the music industry dictate that a holiday record must arrive in stores several shopping weeks before the merriest season rolls 'round. Therefore, the master tapes must be delivered to the pressing plant months in advance. So like diligent elves...the artist, composers, lyricists, producers, arrangers, and engineers convene in short-sleeve shirts and sandals to create musical landscapes of drifting snow and winter wonderlands.

In 1966, when it came time for Barbra to choose material for her now classic *A Christmas Album*, she took—as usual—the road less traveled. For mixed in with the lovely "White Christmas" and *chestnuts roasting's*, were such diverse selections as "My Favorite Things" (from Rodgers and Hammerstein's *The Sound of Music*—now considered a Christmas standard); a new song, "The Best Gift" (in celebration of her soon-to-be-born son, Jason); *Gounod*'s "Ave Maria"; and the sublime "I Wonder As I Wander." For many, the highlight was a romping, jazzy "Jingle Bells," where Barbra deconstructed the traditional nursery rhyme/Christmas party tempo—turning it into something completely her own. *A Christmas Album* went on to sell millions of copies and has re-entered the charts every year since its first release. Its timeless artistry has become as much a part of the holidays as eggnog and mistletoe.

All of the *greats* have made Christmas records—Bing Crosby, Frank Sinatra, Judy Garland, Ella Fitzgerald, Nat King Cole, Elvis Presley, and Johnny Mathis, to name a few...each of them associated with quintessential standards. While it's daunting to improve upon that kind of perfection, every December finds scores of artists from all genres—rock to jazz...country to cabaret—making new contributions to the canon of holiday releases.

For Barbra, the creative challenge of this collection is, once again, balancing the traditional with the contemporary...finding something unique to express...discovering melodies and lyrics in newer songs which can easily rest beside the acknowledged standards...seeking untapped beauty in the oft-visited evergreens. Being mostly drawn to material which evokes a bitter-sweet, wistful longing, she's chosen to interpret the work of several of the best practitioners of popular song—Johnny Mandel, Alan & Marilyn Bergman, Don Costa, Frank Loesser, Stephen Sondheim, and others. As Sondheim did in the past, with lyric additions to Barbra's remarkable versions of "Send In the Clowns," "Putting It Together," and "I'm Still Here"...he now revisits an earlier composition, "I Remember." With a new opening verse, this plaintive soliloquy from his television musical *Evening Primrose* has been transformed into a subtly haunting remembrance of Christmas's past.

It's interesting to note that 35 years ago when Barbra recorded *A Christmas Album* she was just getting over a cold and feeling rather hoarse. Although the casual listener might not have noticed, the slight huskiness in her voice imbued the songs with a burnished glow, rendering them all the more intimate. Today however, she's singing with even greater richness, clarity, and golden tone than ever before. Her enormous breadth of artistic and life experience—as stage and screen actress, film director, record producer, songwriter...singer...mother and wife—now informs these songs with all the meaning intended (and hoped for) by the writers...plus that something extra—known in certain circles as divine inspiration.

In this day and age when the true spirit of the holidays is sometimes lost amidst a frenzy of commercialization, it's nice to know that certain gifts will last beyond the greeting cards and colorful wrapping paper. Some things are of *our* time...and some are for *all* time. This disc is one of those—music to enjoy not only at Christmas, but throughout the year...a precious expression from the heart—by one of creation's greatest gifts...Barbra Streisand.

—Jay Landers

Contents

I'll Be Home for Christmas

Words and Music by
Kim Gannon and Walter Kent

Moderately slow

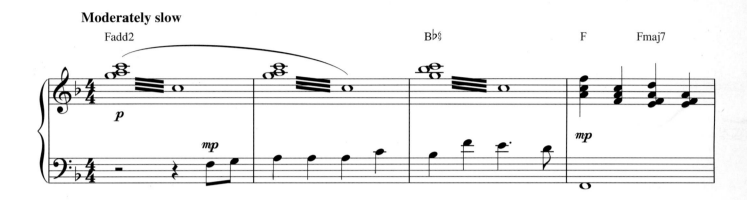

I'm dream-ing ____ to-night of a place I love ____ e - ven

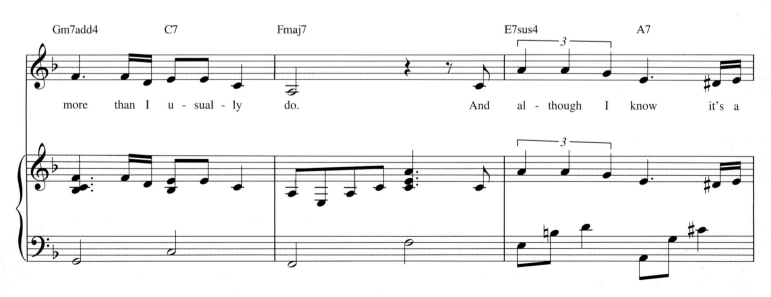

more than I u-sual-ly do. And al-though I know it's a

A Christmas Love Song

Lyric by
Alan Bergman and Marilyn Bergman

Music by Johnny Mandel

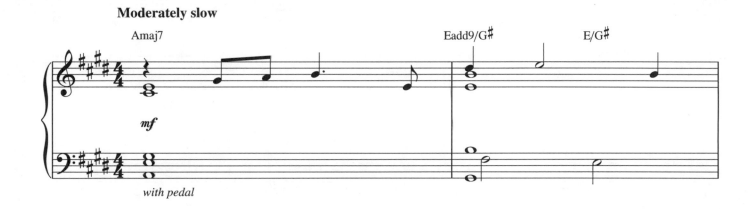

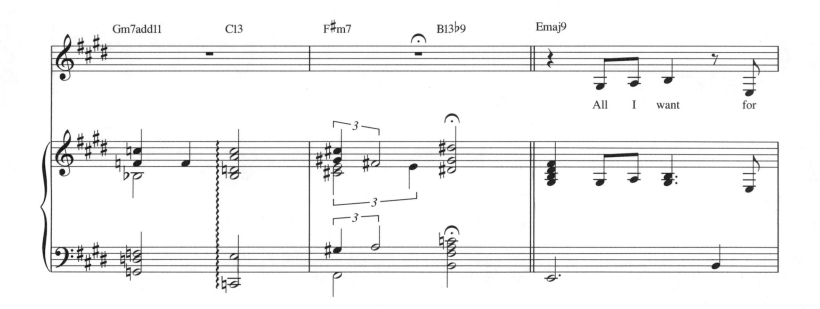

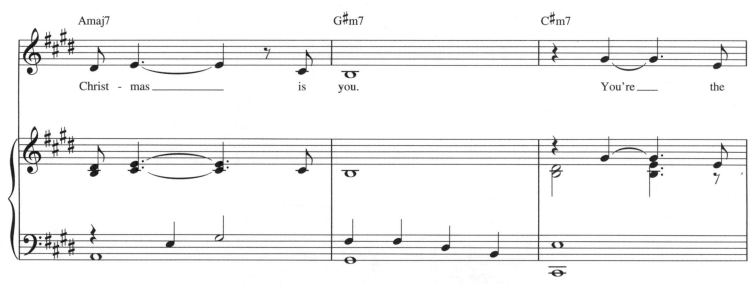

or _____ the tin - sel's _____ sil - ver glow,

you just _____ have to look at me and, oh,

Christ - mas _____ is here! _____

What Are You Doing New Year's Eve?

By Frank Loesser

New Year's Eve?

Maybe I'm crazy to suppose that you'd choose me. Ah, but in case I stand one little chance,

I Remember

Words and Music by
Stephen Sondheim

leaves.

I re-mem-ber leaves,

green as spear-mint, crisp as pa-per. I re-mem-ber

trees, bare as coat racks, spread like bro-ken um-

brel-las. And parks, and bridg-es, ponds, and zoos.

Snow Bound

Words and Music by
Russell Faith and Clarence Kehner

Un - a - fraid, un - a - fraid, _____ snow - bound to -

geth - er, _____ here ____ with love ____

____ locked ____ in our arms. ____

And if the world _____ nev - er should find us, ____

It Must Have Been the Mistletoe
(Our First Christmas)

By Justin Wilde and Doug Konecky

*Recorded a half step higher.

had his fin - gers crossed_____ that we would fall in love.___ It

must have___ known that kiss would lead to all of this._____ It

must have been___ the mis - tle - toe,___ the la - zy fire,___ the fall - ing snow,___ the

mag - ic___ in the frost - y air,___ that made me love___ you.___ On

Christmas Lullaby

Words and Music by
Ann Hampton Callaway

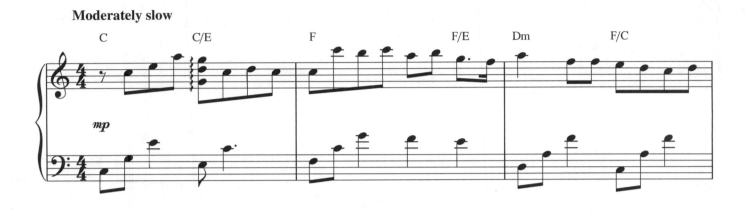

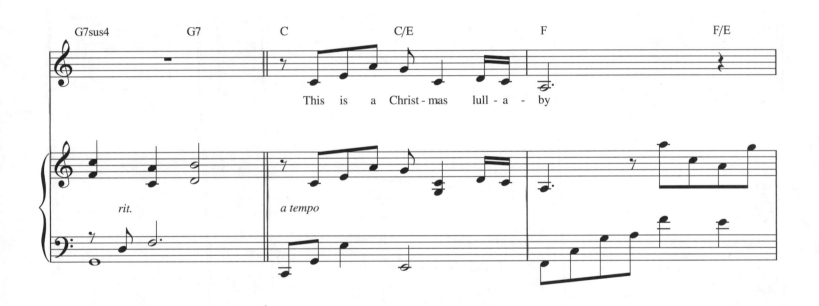

Christmas Mem'ries

Words by
Alan Bergman and Marilyn Bergman

Music by Don Costa

Moderately slow

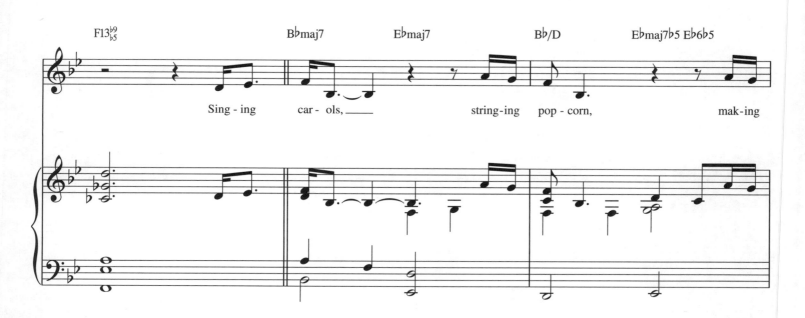

Sing - ing car - ols, _____ string-ing pop - corn, mak-ing

Coda

Eb/F   F/Eb   Dm7   Ab13   F/G   Bb13   Bb9#5

Christ - mas   I've ev - er   known. _____   Sing - ing _____

Ebmaj7   Ab13#11   Ab9/Gb   Bb/F

car - ols,   string-ing pop-corn,   shin - y fac - es of all the

G13sus4   G13 Db9#11   Cm9   Eb/F   F13

chil - dren. _____ Pre - cious mem - 'ries, _____   of ev - 'ry Christ - mas   I've

Eb6/9   Bbadd9/D   Cm9   F7sus4 Bmaj13 Bbmaj13

known. _____

Grown-Up Christmas List

Words and Music by
David Foster and Linda Thompson-Jenner

Slowly, freely

you re-mem-ber me? I sat up-on your knee. I wrote to you ___ with child-hood fan-ta-

sies. Well, I'm all grown up now. Can you still help some-how? I'm

* Recorded a half step higher.

Moderately slow, in time

ways ___ win, and love would nev - er ___ end. ___

This is my grown - up ___ Christ - mas list. This is my on - ly life - long ___

wish. ___ This is ___ my grown - up ___ Christ - mas list. ___

Mm, ___ mm ___ mm.

Ave Maria

Arranged by William Ross

53

dic - ta tu in mu - li - e - ri - bus, et

be - ne - dic - tus, et

be - ne - dic - tus fruc - tus ven - tris, ven - tris

tu - i, Je - sus.

54

Closer

Music and Lyrics by
Tom Snow and Dean Pitchford

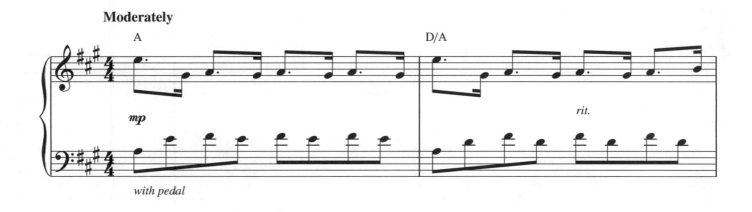

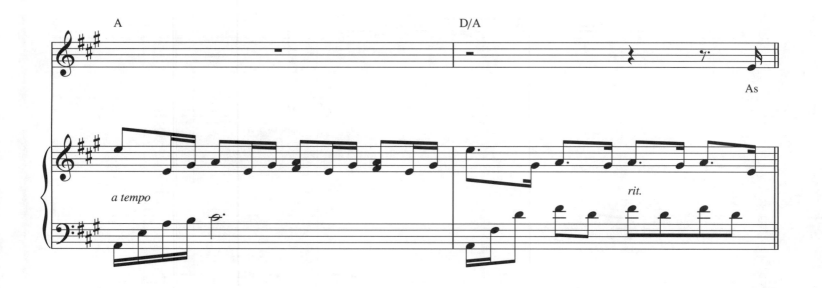

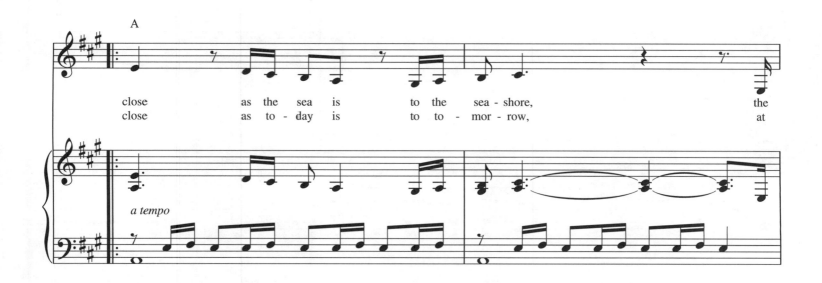

close ... as the sea is ... to the sea-shore, ... the
close ... as to-day is ... to to-mor-row, ... at

close   as the glow is   to the em - ber, _____   you've
sure   as the snow - fall   in De - cem - ber, _____   your

al - ways   been a ____   part ____ of me.
love lives   on in ____   ev - 'ry - thing.

Now liv - ing in my heart   you're e - ven clos - er, _____

clos - er. _____

63

One God

Words and Music by
Ervin M. Drake and James Shirl

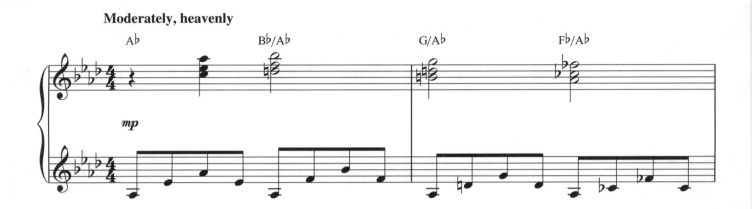

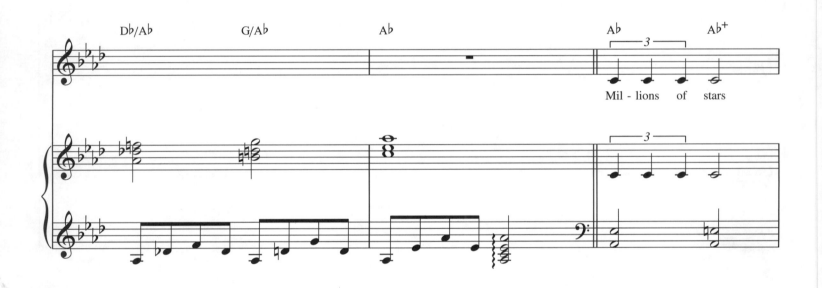

Mil - lions of stars

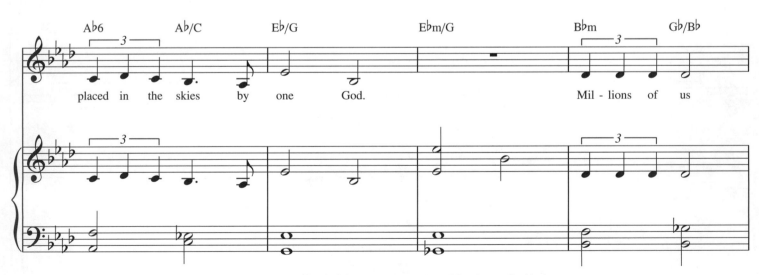

placed in the skies by one God.

Mil - lions of us

one. _____
(Mil - lions of stars placed in the skies by one God.)

One God. (Mil - lions of us lift up our eyes to

one God.) One God. So man - y chil - dren call - ing out loud by

man - y a dif - f'rent ___ name. _____ One

there were no stran- gers af- ter the work was ___ done. _____ Now

our God, _____ yes, your ___ God, _____ and
(Our God.) (Your God.)

my God _____ are ___ one. _____

great songs series

Cherry Lane Music is proud to present this legendary series which has delighted players and performers for generations.

Great Songs of the Fifties

The latest release in Cherry Lane's acclaimed Great Songs series, this songbook presents 51 musical memories from the fabulous '50s! Features rock, pop, country, Broadway and movie tunes, including: All Shook Up • At the Hop • Blue Suede Shoes • Dream Lover • Fly Me to the Moon • Kansas City • Love Me Tender • Misty • Peggy Sue • Rock Around the Clock • Sea of Love • Sixteen Tons • Take the "A" Train • Wonderful! Wonderful! • and more. Includes an introduction by award-winning journalist Bruce Pollock.

_____02500323 P/V/G.............................$16.95

Great Songs of the Sixties, Vol. 1 – Revised Edition

The newly updated version of this classic book includes 80 faves from the 1960s: Angel of the Morning • Bridge over Troubled Water • Cabaret • Different Drum • Do You Believe in Magic • Eve of Destruction • Georgy Girl • It Was a Very Good Year • Monday, Monday • People • Spinning Wheel • Walk on By • and more.

_____02509902 P/V/G.............................$19.95

Great Songs of the Sixties, Vol. 2 – Revised Edition

61 more 60s hits: And When I Die • California Dreamin' • Crying • The 59th Street Bridge Song (Feelin' Groovy) • For Once in My Life • Honey • Little Green Apples • MacArthur Park • Me and Bobby McGee • Nowhere Man • Piece of My Heart • Sugar, Sugar • You Made Me So Very Happy • and more.

_____02509904 P/V/G.............................$19.95

Great Songs of the Seventies – Revised Edition

This super collection of 70 big hits from the '70s includes: After the Love Has Gone • Afternoon Delight • Annie's Song • Band on the Run • Cold as Ice • FM • Imagine • It's Too Late • Layla • Let It Be • Maggie May • Piano Man • Shelter from the Storm • Superstar • Sweet Baby James • Time in a Bottle • The Way We Were • more!

_____02509917 P/V/G.............................$19.95

Prices, contents, and availability subject to change without notice.

Great Songs of the Seventies – Volume 2

Features 58 outstanding '70s songs in rock, pop, country, Broadway and movie genres: American Woman • Baby, I'm-A Want You • Day by Day • Do That to Me One More Time • Dog & Butterfly • Don't Cry Out Loud • Dreamboat Annie • Follow Me • Get Closer • Grease • Heard It in a Love Song • I'll Be There • It's a Heartache • The Loco-Motion • My Eyes Adored You • New Kid in Town • Night Fever • On and On • Sing • Summer Breeze • Tonight's the Night • We Are the Champions • Y.M.C.A. • and more. Includes articles by Cherry Lane Music Company founder Milt Okun, and award-winning music journalist Bruce Pollock.

_____02500322 P/V/G.............................$19.95

Great Songs of the Eighties – Revised Edition

This newly revised edition features 50 songs in rock, pop & country styles, plus hits from Broadway and the movies! Songs: Almost Paradise • Angel of the Morning • Do You Really Want to Hurt Me • Endless Love • Flashdance...What a Feeling • Guilty • Hungry Eyes • (Just Like) Starting Over • Let Love Rule • Missing You • Patience • Through the Years • Time After Time • Total Eclipse of the Heart • and more.

_____02502125 P/V/G.............................$18.95

Great Songs of the Nineties

This terrific collection features 48 big hits in many styles. Includes: Achy Breaky Heart • Beautiful in My Eyes • Believe • Black Hole Sun • Black Velvet • Blaze of Glory • Building a Mystery • Crash into Me • Fields of Gold • From a Distance • Glycerine • Here and Now • Hold My Hand • I'll Make Love to You • Ironic • Linger • My Heart Will Go On • Waterfalls • Wonderwall • and more.

_____02500040 P/V/G.............................$16.95

Great Songs of the Pop Era

Over 50 hits from the pop era, including: Amazed • Annie's Song • Ebony and Ivory • Every Breath You Take • Hey Nineteen • I Want to Know What Love Is • I'm Every Woman • Just the Two of Us • Leaving on a Jet Plane • My Cherie Amour • Raindrops Keep Fallin' on My Head • Rocky Mountain High • This Is the Moment • Time After Time • (I've Had) the Time of My Life • What a Wonderful World • and more!

_____02500043 Easy Piano $16.95

™
CHERRY LANE
MUSIC COMPANY
6 East 32nd Street, New York, NY 10016

Quality in Printed Music

Visit Cherry Lane on the Internet at
www.cherrylane.com

EXCLUSIVELY DISTRIBUTED BY

HAL•LEONARD®
CORPORATION

7777 W. BLUEMOUND RD. P.O. BOX 13819 MILWAUKEE, WI 53213

0402

Celebrate Christmas

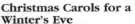

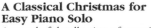

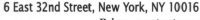

More Great Piano/Vocal Books from Cherry Lane

For a complete listing of Cherry Lane titles available, including contents listings, please visit our web site at

www.cherrylane.com

See your local music dealer or contact:

CHERRY LANE MUSIC COMPANY
6 East 32nd Street, New York, NY 10016

EXCLUSIVELY DISTRIBUTED BY
HAL•LEONARD® CORPORATION
7777 W. BLUEMOUND RD. P.O. BOX 13819 MILWAUKEE, WI 53213

Prices, contents and availability subject to change without notice.

0402